CHAPTER 1
METHODS TO GENERATE WEBSITE TRAFFIC

Developing just a website on the web does not make much sense these days. With the increasing number of websites worldwide individual websites all suffer from decreasing visitors if they get any at all. Webmasters try different techniques to attract visitors to their websites and gradually these techniques have emerged into strategies that people use in order to generate traffic on a regular basis. Although according to the philosophy that if more visitors arriving on your website this would result in more conversion from visitors to customers, but then generating traffic on the website is just not enough to convert the visitors into customers, rather it requires smart techniques to attract only relevant or potential visitors on your website. Many marketing forums and blogs communicate various strategies to generate more traffic to your site, but it is important to figure out which strategies work for you and your web business.

There are various ways that can generate potential traffic to your websites, some of these may seem awkward in implementing but at the end of the day if these techniques are implemented perfectly, they can be highly productive. Some of the major web traffic generation strategies are discussed as under:

Method # 1- Public Recognition

Public recognition of the websites is a good way to generate traffic. In this kind of strategy you actually create awareness about your website which eventually reaches the potential visitors who visit your website. Public Recognition is a broader term, as several strategies have emerged which include website banner exchange, social media pages, and viral marketing. Moreover Public Recognition is also possible through Press Release. Press Releases can give massive spotlight to your website.

Method # 2- Classified Advertisement

Many marketing professionals have discouraged to use promotional techniques like posting free classified advertisement to your website. However, there are some tools of the trade that can work best for your business. Offering free classified posting on your website can generate great amount of potential traffic if applied with good effective techniques.

Method # 3- Blogs

Blog posting is a widely used mode of creating back-links to your site that also supports your website ranking on search engines. However it is important to be cautious because web masters do dislike spamming.

Method # 4- Posting on Craigslist

Although many web developers have misused Craigslist to generate traffic to their sites in the past, but if used smartly, it is a productive method of attracting visitors and can help you a lot in providing good quality traffic.

Method # 5 - Promotional Game

Are you the one who is selling your own product? Then this lesson will work best for you. For promotional activity you can distribute your product to well known marketers or marketing forum to get publicity and good word of mouth popularity. Eventually this will increase traffic to your site. But for this to happen you have to confirm the quality of your product and ensure that it's of competitive standard.

Method # 6- Subscribers

This last lesson has gained great amounts of popularity among the web developers. The unique feature of this method is building and maintaining long term profitable relationship with your visitors. Of all the traffic generation methods, this precise system is well known for not only attracting new visitors but also sustaining them for future and this correlation is mutually beneficial.

Method # 7- Link Exchanges

A widely used methodology from recent past by the marketers from all over the world- reciprocal link exchange is presently also a productive method attracting visitors to your website. This technique works in a 3 way linking system or through driving the traffic from the authority sites to your sites.

From this chapter you have learned seven basic lessons to generate traffic to your site. However, the technique for building high volume traffic to your site is not limited to these seven lessons but in fact they provide you with broad guidelines. These guidelines when applied can be beneficial to your online business.

CHAPTER 2
WHAT IS LINK EXCHANGE?
GENERATE

With the advent of dot com world, links were a simple and straight forward path to assist visitors in finding desired information on the website. With the passage of time and innovations in the internet arena, the importance of links grew much stronger. Many search engines were developed due to which the significance of links grew among webmasters than in visitors.

The importance of links grew when Google initiated the concept of "Page Rank". This Page Rank was basically system of website categorization on the grounds of its significance and pertinence to the subject matter. Google's idea was that the site and the links that points that site are both important. The popularity of sites increases when the link pointing to that site bares sound fame and importance among the visitors.

Therefore, "Page Rank" has gained a significant amount of importance and if you want to have more relevant information on your website you will choose the best link exchange partner so that your visitor doesn't get lost in this global information network.

This will ultimately increase the importance and view ability of your site.

Link exchange or as you may say link partnering is beneficial to your online business in two core forms:-

i. **Traffic Generation Source:** Link exchange will increase the volume of visitors to your website as it will be clicked more placed with relevant exchanges.

ii. **Search Engine Exposure:** Your website will have increased exposure on search engines as it's located with specific keywords.

Generating Traffic for the beginners

The new web master will be more anxious to getting traffic to their site. For this reason in the initial few months new sites can get the borrowed traffic from other websites. They can bargain with different relevant websites to post their links which can give them a way to grab more visitors.

Improving Search Engine Exposure

Search engines are an important source of

providing incoming links or back links. These search engines certify your website by posting your link of their website. This patronage is carried forward in search engine or page ranking. This long way forwarding link from one site to the next passes the page rank without harming its own ranking. This in turn will benefit both back links and search engines. Firstly by increasing page rank of back links and escalating the standard of search engine and secondly by helping the back links sites gets more targeted traffic.

Now you must be wondering how to get back links? Well, this depends on the methodology adopted either you are going for pure back links or reciprocal links. Any of the strategies taken up is made applicable via expresslinking.com. Back links in whatever form are basically favors. More effective links considered are pure back links and forward links.

Both links, one way links and reciprocal links are discussed below.

One way Links

When you post a link on other site on which you don't require any return. This is done when your site is linked by article, request, directories or citation. Expresslinking.com can be effective source of getting this link by signing into it and it accepts its subscriber into accepting the link without any codes of reciprocal links.

Reciprocal Links

As the name says exchange links with other sites. In this type of link an agreement is set with mutual consent. Expresslinking.com provides an easy way out for this task.

Identify Link Partners

To identify link partners the best way is to look for relevant niche websites. The online business with like business type will be fruitful to add link in e.g. your business niche is gifts for example then going or associating with courier business will be beneficial option.

Be Creative

You have to browse sites which have similar keywords as yours. Building exchange partner relationship with such sites would be valuable. Mark the potential 20 sites with similar keywords on their website and make them link exchange partners. For an easier and quicker way of getting link exchange is *express linking*. They provide high quality links where reciprocal link exchange management is also available.

CHAPTER 3
LINK EXCHANGE PRINCIPLES

As mentioned in chapter one, of the most effective traffic building strategy is through Link Exchange. It is the process in which banners and images are exchanged among website owners to market each other, resulting in greater probability of being viewed due to greater advertising. Therefore link exchanges are known to be most productive way of advertising your product.

Customarily, link exchange is free of charge. Since, it results in mutual benefit for the website owners. But nowadays due to the importance of Page Ranking it has taken a different business perspective.

You must be inquisitive as to why web masters are now charging you for offering link exchange? The answer is simple, the degree of their popularity is far greater than yours and by offering you link exchange they are sharing their success.

Before you go for any link exchange agreement there are two key principles that you should adhere to. "Be Vigilant" and "Be Patient".

Being Vigilant

Theme comparability of websites is prerequisite. The ideas and content discussed in target websites should relate to that of yours. If the core ideas differ then you should have closer look at them as it alters the page ranking because Google will detect the resemblance between links based on themes. The detection will be based on the words used in the website content. If the target website doesn't have the same theme, then your ranking will be dependent upon the number of visitors to your site, not by Google and you can ensure your success by getting a million different clinks which is very unlikely for a new business with restricted access to link exchange.

Being Patient

Finding a free link exchange partner requires from a great deal of patience. You need to be aware of various forums used for link exchange because chances are you might find someone with the same names. The websites that have higher ranking than yours would form an appropriate link exchange. If you go for link exchange with a website that has lower ranking then yours, it could bring down your ranking. The norm is to find someone whose ranking is equivalent or higher than yours so collectively you may succeed in PR.

As a marketing tool, link exchanges can play a crucial role in success and in no time at all your site could be among the top sites for a particular topic. All you need is patience when looking for a partner and being vigilant for your specific needs.

CHAPTER 4
DIFFERENTIATING LINK
EXCHANGE SPAM

The notion of link exchange begins to jeopardize with the interference of spam. These spams spread in the internet world like a virus. They browse through the internet, looking for contact info for potential link partner and contact them by sending spam emails.

You must be wondering how these spam emails spreads so fast? Imagine you own 30 sites, which is quite common these days and through contact forms you get 2-10 link exchange spam emails or messages per day on each site. This means you will be getting 60-300 spam messages each day. This is pretty huge volume of messages for which you cannot even promise that these will be relevant. All they ask for is to build link exchange partners irrespective of their relevance and competence to your online business.

Confronted with collectively 60-300 spam messages on average is it a hassle. You will surely not be prone to go through all these messages when the probability for their relevance is very low. 80%-90% of such messages are insignificant so the first thing you will be doing to these messages is selecting them all and clicking delete.

This automatic link building can be beneficial to some businesses but due to their low quality and low relevance to the potential client they are generally considered to be ineffective.

If you are looking for an alternative to build quality a link exchange partner and yet be automated you have to think out of box and be creative. One such logical and creative way of doing this is through website designated for special link building partners. They do it very smartly with high quality and relevance. There are also many websites that ask for full information about your websites for link exchanges. These are in every way better than to astray from targeted business.

Now if you compare both the alternatives of getting link partners, you will see that the probability of getting productive outcome from special link building solutions is 80% more than spam messages. Whereas on the other hand these spam messages get ignored 80-90% and who knows 10-20% of these messages will be productive.

The system of using special link building

solutions can have one disadvantage, it needs manual work. But this can be technically solved by simply copying and pasting your site information into link exchange submission forms and repeat for all your websites. For automation you can create link exchange directories with sites having relevant text of every particular category. Besides this, automation can be created through less files, SEO and back links checking. With this automation links can be created without sacrificing on quality.

When you come across people complaining about automated link exchange quality then you will be sure that they are unaware of their creativity and rationality behind its success. The methodology mentioned works best and it is evident when your site ranks on the first page in Google search engine. Many people have benefited from this strategy and you will be the next successful player of the game.

Internet marketing is not that easy but to be successfully sustained in this business you have to learn the accurate rules of the game and be creative. You can add value to your online business by expanding it to SEO.

CHAPTER 5
SEARCH ENGINE RANKING AND
LINK EXCHANGE

Link exchange provides a convenient way for high Google rankings if you are using any link exchange software to aid you, or you are increasing your website visibility on your own. It is useful when you want to get a thick net of back links to boost your ranking.

Why exchange links?

It is impossible to imagine success in online business without having strong search engine ranking base for your site. It assures that you are reaching towards your target market, offering what they are looking for at the right time.

Getting to the top of Google ranking list is gaining Google's trust which your competitor might not be entitled to. The building block of developing a trustful relationship is by convincing other website to post a link of your site. These links will increase the value of your site. The more relevant a link is the more valued your site be.

To be successful in the online business you need to get links to increase your website credibility. As web developer gurus proudly acclaim a site to be of high professional standards and rank A1 if it gets quality links. Online business is all about timing. Being at the right place at the right time is very crucial and creating links can take years.

To save time and have quality in your online business, link exchange comes into play. These link exchanges can provide your website with relevant and competent volume of links. The mechanism is simpler than it seems. You and other websites are mutually benefited by posting links on each other websites. This correlation provides support to both and more importantly it builds stronger relationship with Google.

How to get started?

How to exchange links? What steps would be required? Whether to do it on your own or with link exchange software? Before you research for the answers to all these questions, first you need to quest for websites that are similar and close to your business segment. Avoid link trading hubs and networks and don't go for links from websites that post lots of diversified link partners. You should start link exchanges that suit your business with best links which give a competitive edge to your website by increasing its quality standards and pertinence to visitors need.

The next step is to convince the web owner to exchange links with your business. To do so, you have to initiate contact professionally with a formal request, letter or an email to persuade link exchange partner to do business with you. While making a business offer you have to show you are personally interested in the business, being alert and attentive when addressing the web owner by their name and using website address or URL.

While writing to the web owner you will be applying AIDA technique of communication skills. You will be giving all the necessary information about you like your name, your website URL, purpose of writing and the text you will be including in your site. The content should be such that it interests the web owners then they are much likely to do the business with you. Your text should be precise, specific, clear and convincing.

There are many proficient link exchange software applications available in the market. It saves time and your resources as they will provide you with automated process in building link exchanges. While using software you have to be sure that it provides you with email specs or layouts to coordinate your email with partners and save you from any deceiving techniques which might be used by your partner, like disguising accurate page ranks of their sites. When specific software fulfills all these specifications you will definitely see the benefits.

CHAPTER 6
LINK EXCHANGE WEB PROMOTION STRATEGY

The most preferred marketing technique for promoting your website is "Link Exchange". Link exchange will provide links that are directed to your website, increasing the favorable Google votes and benefiting you with ranking on your site.

To get productive outcomes from link exchange mechanism, it's important for you to find out websites that are similar to your business and contain information which you think is of high quality and relevant to your online business. It's also necessary to make sure that specific links should bare sound ranking because the credibility of your website also depends on the standards of the links ranking.

When looking for links it's better to prioritize the links according to their standards. SEO experts have rated high for information sites that contains the edu.com domain. These are the educational sites and are given edu.com domain from government authority therefore their credibility and ranking among other information sites are comparatively high. Linking your website with such domains will endorse the authenticity of the text available on it and visitors can get valuable information from your website. When targeted visitors feel that their information needs are best met through your site, they would maintain a long term relationship with your online business.

After the edu.com domain the second priority is given to main educational sites where browsers usually go for research and information. When for any reason you can't link your website to the edu.com domain then you can link to any of the main educational sites which are highly visited. The best way of choosing the site for link exchange is to jot down all the relevant keywords from your website. Now type these keywords accordingly on the search engine bar. Note the site that appears on the result page. Only set focus on the sites that appear on the first two pages of the search engine. Check the quality, relevance and page rank of these resulting sites. Choose the sites whose literature on the website is most related to your business and whose Page Ranking is higher than yours. You can check the page ranking via PRChecker.info by writing the website URL on the question bar and it will then show you Google Page Ranking.

Web promotional technique is of course not limited to this text but it provides you with the most convenient way of doing online business in the most profitable manner in real time.

CHAPTER 7
FINDING GOOD LINK EXCHANGE PARTNERS

In this chapter we will unveil the ways of hunting Link Exchange Partners. If you are doing business from home then these techniques will help you in making your online business very effective.

The sorted best methods of finding link exchanges are discussed below.

a. Search portals are lucrative gateways of finding link exchanges. You can start up by listing the possible keywords, searching them through the search engine and then ultimately noting the possible URL, site or link from the most recent result.

b. Observing competitors is always worthwhile. Know your competitors links because these can also be advantageous to your business.

c. Looking for link exchange tools. Several websites have similar content as yours and would like to be business partners with you. Best two link exchange partners are Linkalizer and sitesell's

a. value exchange. Avoid links that automate the process completely as search engines might not accept such links.

b. For ease and sparing time there is software that can assist you in finding Link Exchange and will inform you by sending an email. One such good option is Link Assistant. While using this you need to be watchful of spam messages.

These methods will help you in finding best link exchange partner for your home based business to be successful.

CHAPTER 8
CHOOSING GOOD LINK EXCHANGE PARTNERS

Now that you have learned that Link Exchange Partnering is one of the most effective promotional strategies. It's about time you make a wise decision in choosing the best links for your website. While selecting the website for back links you need to be creative, watchful and rational.

Following lessons will help you to select the best link exchange partners for your online business.

Lesson # 1 Link Popularity and its Contents

The popularity of the links is measured by means of Google page rank. Higher the rank of a page, greater would be its popularity. For link exchanges websites with higher ranks will be preferred. But you will certainly not limit yourself on the rank for judging website credibility. Read and evaluate thoroughly the contents and quality of material presented on the site. You might get good and relevant information from unfamiliar site that ranks 2/10 and it's possible that you get junk from site rating 8/10. Therefore, besides considering the site popularity through its ranks the relevance and significance of contents on the web is also judged.

Lesson # 2 Unwanted Reciprocal Links

In link exchange there is a threat of unwanted reciprocal sites that gets linked to your website unintentionally. The low quality of reciprocal links can portray a bad impression on your website and give your site a lower ranking. You will prefer the website that has relevant information along with decent ranking so your site visitors are benefited with quality information.

Lesson # 3 Don't Link for the Sake of Linking

Any fame is better than no fame, doesn't fit with the online business. For creating link exchange partners, owners have to create back links that are doing similar business. You want to have information on your website which is beneficial to your visitor and they would refer to your site whenever involve in research. To have top notch website links you would answer the basic questions like:

i. What is the information you would be offering to your visitor?

i.   Which topics would be covered in your contents?
ii.   When and where would your links be exchange with other sites?
iii.   How else will you be moving forward for your link popularity?

Lesson # 4 Look for Relevant Sites

To link your website with relevant sites you can list them with search engines and the directories. Getting competitor information will also help in building productive links. Knowing your customers policy also goes well with knowing your competitor strategy. The link partners they have buildup can also have link exchange partnership with your online business, and also assures they accept website listing of your online business. To increase the popularity of your website add credentials like biography of the author, website links, copyright information and reprint information about your company. These small things can aid in exceptional web promotion.

Lesson # 5 Put yourself in Customer's Shoes!

Google search engine can help in attracting high volumes of visitors to your site. You need to add special features to create a unique selling preposition (USP) to get a competitive edge. Your core competencies will be focused on quality contents, better navigation, user friendly features, code validity and relevance. So that search engine gives the best result.

Lesson # 6 Is to Work Hard.

Last but not least, working hard is anyway better than finding loop holes. Key to success in online business is that besides your creativity and rational thinking you need to work hard to continuously improve yourself. Capitalize on keyword application on the search engine. Don't ignore basic instincts in search of philosophical ideas.

These lessons will help you in building sustainable link exchange partner where probability of success will be far greater than the failure of your online business.

CHAPTER 9
THE RECIPROCAL LINK EXCHANGE

You can't deny with the effectiveness of Reciprocal links and the popularity of your website. Although many web developers prefer one way links over reciprocal link exchange but reciprocal link exchange is productive in getting traffic to your site. In getting reciprocal link exchange for new web developers, it gets difficult for them to get links on the websites with high page rank as their page rank in the beginning is very low.

This is the major dispirit element for new web developers who have invested their time and resources in developing websites and sorting relevant websites with high page rank. Therefore to be successful and popular in the online business, new entrants can follow the following systematic approach that will enable them to produce positive results and be successful.

Step # 1 Do Your Home Work

Most importantly before looking for link exchange, you need to do your home work first. Your website should be complete and accurate. The literature on your site should be of high quality, relevant to the subject matter of your website and serves all the information needs of your customer/visitor. To have good search engine preference among all other websites focus on keywords strengthening.

Step # 2 Register with Search Engine

When you have optimized your site with keyword/keywords, register your site with premier search engine like Yahoo, Google, MSN, Alta Vista etc. only submit your site when its complete and you are satisfied that the content and it's of high quality standards. Avoid presenting sites "Under Construction". Websites in this state will further delay indexing.

Step # 3 Acquiesce with Directories

Knock down your website with specialized directories like open directories, Yahoo, Joe Ant and more of such prominent ones. Directories are classified in three categories; you need to select which one to go for to have maximum results. Three different types of directories include:-

a. Directories offering free listing without any reciprocal linking
b. Directories offering free listing but with reciprocal linking
c. Directories offering only paid listing.

As paid listings can be costly for the new web developer therefore as new entrants in the internet world you can opt for the option of free listing on the directories with high page rank. This will give you economical promotional strategy where your website will be exposed to more one link and reciprocal link in the dot com world and will increase the popularity and significance of your online business.

Step # 4 Publicizing Your Website

In your systematic approach of creating links by posting your website on directories you can start writing about the concept of your website and what purpose it serves, focusing on its main features and keywords and how it creates convenience to your customer. This literature can take the form of articles and can be published on article banks, article directories or any channel of article distribution. Your website gains popularity when your articles are connected with links with high page ranking.

Since it's an important source of getting productive links to your website, some tips are underlined below that will assist you to come up with some quality material.

Tip # 1: Concentrate on quality. The subject

matter, language and your gestures in article should portray your professional expertise in the internet business.

Tip # 2: the idea behind writing articles is getting one way links that will increase visitor traffic to your site in the quickest possible way, and will make you prominent member of online business galaxy. Therefore to have a fast link, your site should include contact link at the end of your article that points the direct link to your website for visitors.

Tip # 3: If you don't possess the competences to bring up a good quality article that can give you successful results then stop wasting your time in writing and outsource this task to some better writers which will be resourceful to your online business.

Step # 5: Posting Recommendations at Forums

Recognize your site expert opinion by posting them on concerned discussion forums ingrained with your endorsement and URL. Request the web master to publish testimonials written by you about products and services you have used and add links of your website to augment its popularity.

Step # 6: Request for Reciprocal Link Exchange

These strategic steps will increase the rank of your page from 2, 3 to even 4. It's the time when your site is climbing the ladder of success and popularity. It will be well recommended and recognize by well known search engines, web directories and also by web developers who must have gone through your articles and post on related forums. It's about time when you will be requesting for highly ranked reciprocal link exchanges. Make choices from sites that rank higher than yours and are listed at the category of PR 5 or may be PR 6.

At this point you will be thinking why many expert web developers would not like to link with your site. Because now you possess three major USP that gives your site a competitive edge and any of a superior ranked web developer would like to be associated with your link. The three USP you have gained are:

   a. Reasonably high Page Rank
   b. Having a position of expert in the internet business.
   c. You have competed over others on your contents and quality of information in your site which internet expert has also accredited.

The systematic steps presented in this chapter will enable your online business to get high quality link exchange partners from which you can enjoy a reasonably sound position in the internet world.

CHAPTER 10
MANAGING THE LINK EXCHANGE
REQUESTS

As you have learned in the previous chapters that exchanging links is a way of increasing traffic to your website and choosing these link partners is a critical element. For this you have to consider the importance and relevance of content to your own business type. Websites with high page rank are preferred for a links tradeoff. While undergoing this process of link exchanges, there is one thing for which you need to be watchful and that is of being deceived. There are many web owners in the dot com world would cheat you or have already cheated you.

It is surprising but true, "Page Ranking can be False!" yes you must be perplexed with this but it's the harsh reality of online business genre. Brick and mortar businesses are betrayed through fiendish deeds of rivals, in the internet world web owners also cheat you by showing fake page ranking to attract your linkages and their popularity. These cheat do this by fraudulently getting high ranks like # 4 in Google and then email you for link exchanges.

When you receive such emails you can

confirm the ranking by using a simple fire fox plug-in called search status, it will show the page rank of desired URL. But the actual picture gets revealed when you actually visit the website. The quality of the contents in the website can give you an idea; does this website deserve the rank it owns? You will be able to judge whether you are cheated or not?

Now the question that might be popping in your mind would be how would I get to know that I'm being cheated? Don't worry and just be vigilant and focus on the two elementary tips given below. They can save you from great loss which you have not imagined.

Tip # 1

The first rule of the game is websites with high page ranking will obviously have lots of links on their site. You can check these links from Alexa. Page rank of your page is higher than the back links on your site will be greater. Therefore if the website claiming to have high page ranking and doesn't have any or enough back links then PR of that site is doubtful and can be considered as fake.

Tip # 2

To check the authenticity of the website ranking just type on the Google page "info.

Domain name". After typing this, the result doesn't show the website you have type in the domain name prefixing "info", then the high page ranking is doubtful and you have been cheated with fake PR.

For increasing traffic to your website Exchange links is a productive tool. Therefore when using exchange links as a promotional strategy you have to be cautious and sure about the credibility of the links posted because you can any time be cheated in the Internet world.

CHAPTER 11
THREE WAY LINK EXCHANGE
CONCEPT

In today's online business organization, the success and failure of any website is evaluated by the volume of traffic the site receives. High page ranking sites receive higher traffic as such sites rank high in the most prominent search engines.

As you have learned in previous chapters to get good page rank you need to have quality back links from websites with high trustworthiness. These back links should have a page ranking equal or usually better than yours and are doing business in the same segment. For creating value to your website relevance and merit, contacts and back links are very important. These back links are usually created by reciprocal link exchanges. Reciprocal links are created when two websites are linked with each other. There is no particular harm with reciprocal links except that it's not valued by Google. Finding one way link is very difficult, and then come the role of three way linking.

Whenever Google's spider discover a link on a page, it examines it to see if its links to and fro. If Google detects it to have reciprocal link exchange it will use complicated algorithm that will lower the ranking of both pages. Creating three way linking is beneficial and saves your site to be downgraded.

Creating Three Way link

In creating a three way linking system, three web developers form a connecting network where 1 link is connected with 2nd and 2nd with 3rd. The last 3rd link then connects itself with the first. There is no reciprocal linking so Google can't detect the exchange and site can maintain and increase its ranking. To get started with three way link exchange you will be required two web developers to get into an exchange with your website. You can even use software to get this task done for you. It will take minimum time and you will have high volume of traffic to your site through quality back links.

Why to go for three way links?

The system of three way link exchange is innovative and dynamic. Along with increased traffic to your site, it will generate stream of cash flow for your online business to run sustainably. One of the critical aspects like all other businesses, in the web world there is also the threat of going bankrupt. Therefore web developers have to continuously rejuvenate their business offerings and tune their promotional strategies in such a way that they remain in business profitably for longer term.

CHAPTER 12
PROS AND CONS OF LINK EXCHANGE

This chapter discusses some advantages of link exchange and how it can benefit your online business.

Constructive Consequences

Link exchange is ideal for your online business. If you are new in business and have restricted access to internal and external links, link exchange helps you with Page Rank and in no time you will be among the number 1 sites of the search engine. External links not only aid in directing traffic to your site and contributing towards your page rank it also aids in conversions. You should have hands on experience with link exchange if you are interested in conversions.

From a consumer's perspective, links are useful in buying decisions; you can find all the information from the single page, even those about the complimentary products thus aiding you in your choice.

Reciprocal links are helpful to everyone; they all get similar things and need not to bargain over price, because each party is getting their share. That is why link exchange appears to be the most lucrative as well as fair option.

Short comings

One of the most damaging aspects of link exchange is that it directs traffic away or off your site. Too many links posted on your site will divert the visitors' attention from your site and they will be tempted to visit any one of these links. Google doesn't approve link exchanges that end up in simple swaps and considers it to be no more than a junk. They are believed to be similar to off-white SEO.

You can use triangle link system which is better option than simple swap. In this system you use different URL for different links. You should remember that straight links is a big no!

For link exchange partnership to be successful it's important that the links posted on your site should be of high quality and compliments the information presented in your website for the viewers.

This chapter has highlighted major pros and cons of the online business strategies regarding link exchange from which you have to make a wise decision for what suits your business the best. It's important that you are well equipped with all the necessary information, write articles about your business to get feedback and acknowledge the recommendation made on your website. This will help you sail in the boat of successful online business.

CHAPTER 13
USING A LINK EXCHANGE
DIRECTORY

Link exchange directories play a crucial role for your online business repute; it can either increase its popularity or defame it completely. By practicing the appropriate and relevant link exchange methodologies you can ensure outcomes that will benefit you in long term. Desirable link exchange directories would avoid performing exchange of two links among each other, as in the case of link for link result, rather it will opt for one way link.

What is one way link and why is it important?

In one way link, your site will direct link to another site which doesn't direct link back to you. It is an essential factor when establishing website quality. As quality of back links is of paramount importance, the act of placing your link on every possible site and allowing them the same will destruct your websites standing. So you can use a link exchange directory that proposes an associate with the definite need similar to that of yours. One way linking is more productive than reciprocal linking because Google and many other search engines interpret exorbitant usage of reciprocal link as an operation which disrespects webmaster policy.

When you use a link exchange directory for reciprocal link purposes, you have to face many concerns, where on one hand it will make the content of your site un-useful for the targeted audience on the other hand it will also results in blacklisting of your website. To save yourself from such troubles, you are required to confirm from the link exchange directory that all the links in use are one way link. You should maintain the flexibility and vigilance when deciding who you want to link to or who you want to link to you because at the end of the day your motto is to provide germane links to the visitors tailored to their needs.

If you use link exchange directory in a suitable manner it will reward you with quality of back links and will punish if used improperly.

CHAPTER 14
LINK EXCHANGE ETHICS

Quality and relevance of links are imperative pillars for your website prominence. Your website rating and search engine ranking, traffic generating and augmenting revenues are all factors dependent upon the quality and relevance of your link exchange. Many companies on their way to getting success and for competitive position in the internet world engage themselves in unprofessional practices that are not ethically acceptable. Some of such acts observed to be practiced by many web developers are as follows:

a. Searching for quality relevant sites is a time consuming task. Therefore, many of the web developer, being short of time, outsource a leading SEO expert to look for quality relevant sites for them. Companies move on to link exchange sites when these SEO proves to be unproductive. Besides few, most of the link exchange sites didn't give large quantity of good relevant sites. Companies to survive in the cut throat competition, go for advertisements for generating traffic.

a. In the Do It Yourself approach you need to update your web page to check whether reciprocal links no longer exist.

b. Many of the competitors have been using hundreds of links to increase link popularity. When you closely evaluate these links, you will see that many of the back links we found to be from directory and the sites containing insignificant content. Thus all these inbound links were directing from few specified sites.

c. There are many websites that are only built to create link popularity and traffic to their sites. It was well observed by these sites having same outlook, display, color and picture themes. You will observe that these sites were made from 'Related Resources' and your competitor's site must be linked to these sites to increase its page ranking.

d. It has been observed that a company runs several sites with different IP address. It was evident by domain names, ISP and contact information for administrative and technical assistance. It is also seen that even sites with low traffic have high ranking. It is evident by checking on Alexa.com.

These all are practiced by companies which might be your competitor to increase their site popularity and page ranking of their primary business sites. Such a process is done by:

i. Domain name registration that has the keyword similar to your primary business.

ii. Developing a separate hosting account with ISP that has different IP address.

iii. Using the keyword from the primary business sites for the new pages develop in setting up link exchange system.

iv. As these websites are linked together, whenever visitor subscribes to the site it will increase the traffic to both these sites thus resulting in higher page ranking and link popularity.

It has been observed that these practices are neither isolated nor are they wide spread in the internet world, but are used by many companies as a marketing technique. According to some of the web developers, such practices are not considered to be unethical. After all it's simple, cost effective and ultimately increases the rank of website. However, many web developers will have contradictory views as they believe that only honesty can bring long term profitability and sustainability to the business relationships. Therefore, such companies always find ways to abolish these practices. Search engines also adjust their algorithms for such purposes and are starting to sort it out.

one is also a common hindrance to the success of link exchange partners. Many web developers opt for it to avoid any links on their sites. These web developers post their links in frames from sites with no page rank. You will see many of the sites loaded from geocities or other hosts which you cannot easily identify. One convenient method to identify IE is by clicking specified area with the link and click properties. If the web address doesn't counterpart with the address in the bar of your browser then this link is being loaded from other location. Such links are harmful to your website because these are mostly ignored by search engines and you get no popularity out of bearing these links on your site.

Redirect Links

These are not directly harmful to your website but the only problem with them is they are not considered by search engine. You can get popularity through such link exchange if your site has lots of clicks hit to it. The mechanism that works under it is that such link is in CMS system where you will often see your site address to appear like out.php? Id=4095 instead of actual web address scripted on the URL of your site. By clicking this link visitor will be redirected to your website. Therefore redirect links are avoided as they gain no popularity from link exchange agreements.

In doing business as web developers, you should be tied up with strong principles and strategic approach with eagles view in adopting any business strategy for your web development. A small mistake of yours can put you into great trouble which can require your life long income and reputation to recover. The key to success in the online business is to be creative, watchful and well equipped with all the tactics of internet marketing. 40

CHAPTER 16
LINK EXCHANGE-DON'TS

This chapter will discuss some don'ts about link exchange. You must have come across many benefits of link exchange but it is equally important to draw your attention towards actions that you should avoid when it comes to link exchange, as they can proof to be detrimental to website ranking. Even unintentional practices would have harmful effects on your ranking as search engines are extremely particular so it's very crucial to be shrewd when deciding what you should not be doing.

No to Link Farms

Avoid at every cost exchange of links with other farms. A website which appears to be like link farm, say no to it. Your association with the link farm will adversely affect the website ranking eroding away your firm's value.

Words Selection

You should try to avoid possible words that are not relevant to your website. For instance phrase like 'click here' if it has no practical implication or value avoid it from your link.

Remember that you are supposed to use words in text links which are relevant as well as descriptive.

Relevance

You must have come across many people saying 'relevance' counts. As in the case of link exchange this philosophy not only holds true but is very crucial for the promotion of website. You should not participate in link exchange where there is little or no connection between the website. For example if you are running an entertainment website, the ideal link would be a website that has close association with your business instead of linking your websites with business like auto body parts or any mechanical parts.

To have a productive link exchange partnership, besides looking at its positive aspects you should also thoroughly evaluate the don'ts of link exchanges.

In this book you have learned tools of internet marketing and gaining popularity of your site with increased worth of your online business. It started by learning effective ways of getting quality and relevant links to your site with increased volume of traffic. Seven basic lessons are highlighted for building high volume traffic to your site. Namely these lessons were:

- Public Recognition
- Classified Advertisement
- Blogs
- Posting Craigslist
- Promotional Game
- Reciprocal Link Exchanges
- Subscribers

Many search engines have developed with the expansion of internet world. Among the well known search engines we have Google, Yahoo and MSN. Web developers now face the challenge of making their site list on the top in these search engines. To standardize it Google came up with the idea of "Page Rank". This Page Rank categorizes the website on the grounds of its significance and the content of information presented on it. The higher the quality of website information and the relevance of its links, greater would be its page rank.

Websites that have high page ranking will have high volume of traffic and increased popularity. For a website to a have high page ranking, it needs to have greater exposure to search engine websites. Search engines are an important source of generating links or back links to your site. The success of your site will be evaluated by the more times it appears in the results of the search engine bars. For this you need to optimize your site on keywords and relevance of these words to the back links.

The most effective marketing strategy to build traffic to your site is through link exchange. Before you go for any link exchange agreement there are two key principles that you should adhere to. "Be Vigilant" and "Be Patient".

An alternative way of building quality link partners along with an automated system is doing it through a website designated for this task. There are many websites specialized in the link exchange building relationship. Expresslinked.com is one such example.

Selecting the best Link Exchange Partner is very important and a thought provoking stage

of building link exchange relationship. While selecting the website for back links you need to be creative, watchful and rational.
Following lessons were underlined that will help you in getting preeminent link exchange partner for your online business:

Lesson # 1 Link Popularity and its Contents:

Lesson # 2 Unwanted Reciprocal Links:

Lesson # 3 Don't Link for the Sake of Linking!

Lesson # 4 Look for Relevant Sites

Lesson # 5 put you in Customer's Shoe!

Lesson # 6 Is to Work Hard.

These lessons will help you in building sustainable link exchange partner where probability of success will be far greater than the failure of your online business.

For the new web developers it gets difficult to get Reciprocal link exchange with high ranked sites since their ranking in the initial stage is pretty low. Therefore to be successful in getting high quality reciprocal link exchange, new web developers need to focus on doing their part of the job with full sincerity and completeness; register themselves with search engines, directories; write articles about their websites; post recommendations on forums and lastly give a formal professional request for reciprocal link exchange.

There are many companies who post fake page ranking about their sites which might deceive you in your way of selecting optimum link exchange partner. To avoid getting into this trouble, two tips were identified to help you in making a wise decision. The bottom line of both the tips is that you need to check the contents of the links thoroughly and browse through the back links posted on the site. Quality of both will make you evaluate the actual worth of that site.

At times Reciprocal links are discouraged by Google, therefore three way linking systems have been introduced which involves three web developers connected to each other but are not reciprocated.

To become a success in the internet world, there are no lope holes. You have to work hard, be vigilant and creative in all your marketing business strategies.